KU-249-167

RELIGION & THE GODS

ROBERT HULL

W

FRANKLIN WATTS

NEW YORK • LONDON • SYDNEY

First published in 1999 by Franklin Watts,
96 Leonard Street, London EC2A 4XD

Franklin Watts Australia
14 Mars Road, Lane Cove,
NSW 2066

Copyright © Franklin Watts 1999

Series editor: Rachel Cooke
Designer: White Design
Consultant: Dr Anne Millard

A CIP catalogue record for this book
is available from the British Library.

ISBN 0 7496 3295 X

Dewey Classification 938

Printed in Dubai U.A.E.

Acknowledgements:
cover photos: AKG Photo London: top left (Museum
Narodowe, Warsaw/E. Lessing), bottom left
(National Museum of Archeology, Naples/E.Lessing),
right (Delphi Museum/E. Lessing)

AKG Photo, London pp. 6b, 7t (Erich Lessing), 8t,
10b, 20l (National Archeological Museum, Athens/
E. Lessing); 16b (National Museum of Archeology,
Naples/E. Lessing); 22l (Delphi Museum/E. Lessing);
8b, 9t, 16t (Munich, Staatl. Antikenslg & Glyptothek/
E. Lessing); 10t, 29t (Musée Vivenel, Compiegne/
E. Lessing); 12t, 15b, 18t, 19b (Kunsthistoriches
Museum, Vienna/E. Lessing); 12b (Acropolis
Museum, Athens/E. Lessing); 4t, 6b, 13t, 13bl, 14l,
15t, 17, 24l, 24r, 25b, 27t (Musée du Louvre,
Paris/E. Lessing); 9b, 18b, 19t, 28b (British
Museum, London/ E. Lessing); 22r (Vatican
Museums, Rome/E. Lessing); 23t (Slg. Archiv. f. Kunst
& Geschichte); 20r, 25t (Muzeum Narodowe,
Warsaw/E. Lessing); 26t (John Hios); 27b
(Archeological Museum, Istanbul/E. Lessing); 28t
(Izmir Museum, Izmir/E. Lessing); 29b Museum of
the Olympic Games, Olympia/John Hios);

AA Photo Library pp. 13br, 18b, 23b;

e.t. Archive pp. 4b, 5b, 11b, (National Museum,
Athens), 7b (Musée du Louvre, Paris), 26b
(Archeological Museum, Ferrara);

Eye Ubiquitous pp. 5t (E.L. Neil), 11t (J. Waterlow);

Robert Harding p. 6t (T. Gervis);

John Heseltine pp. 2-3;

Rex Features p. 14r (François Marit).

CONTENTS

SUTTON LIBRARIES
AND HERITAGE SERVICES
02071967
SEP 2000

J292.08

RELIGION AND THE GODS

The ancient Greeks were very religious, but in a way that was different from how we see religion today. They had no word for religion and no sacred book like the Bible or the Koran. And they believed in many gods, not just one.

Many gods

With many gods to think about, religion entered every corner of the lives of the ancient Greeks. They held frequent festivals for their gods, and paid their respects to them in everyday moments. Offering a gift by dedicating a small statue in a temple, praying or pouring a little wine to the ground were all ways of showing respect. If the Greeks neglected the gods, the gods might neglect them.

Small statuettes like this acrobat were given as offerings to the gods.

'Humanized' gods

In that way, and others, the Greeks imagined gods as being like humans. The sun god was pictured as a human in a gold chariot that horses hauled across the sky. Each part of the world, each force of nature — winds, rivers, the sea — had its humanized gods.

A group of human-looking gods from a temple near Athens: Zeus, his wife Hera and the twins Apollo and Artemis.

zeal: Our word 'zeal', which means a strong feeling such as love or anger or a passionate enthusiasm for something, comes from a Greek word that means loving religion – *zilos*.

Early times

The names of some of the Greek gods and goddesses were found on clay tablets from Crete dated to about 1400 BC, and relics of their worship – including small figures offered as gifts – have been found on mountain tops there too. In Mycenaean palaces, sacrifices to gods were made on the throne-room hearth. So the Greek gods had 2000 years of continuous worship, before the Christian Romans banned the Greek religion in AD 395.

Myths

'The gods are everywhere,' the Greeks would say. There were hundreds of Greek gods, and as many stories told about them – stories we call 'myths'. Story-tellers often told different versions of the same events. But there were certain beliefs, myths and gods that were shared by all Greeks throughout the ancient world.

■■■ **LEGACY** ■■■

Myths explained natural phenonema like the moon. Hesiod links moonlight with Hecate, also goddess of witchcraft.

Many details about the Greek religion were gathered into the story-poems of Homer and Hesiod. Like encyclopedias, they informed the Greeks about which gods protected humans, what caused natural phenonema, how rituals should be performed, and so on. Over 2,500 years later, they are still read and studied by millions of students the world over.

Aphrodite, goddess of beauty, was said in myth to ride through the sky on a goose or swan.

THE TWELVE OLYMPIANS

The gods, so the ancient Greeks believed, ruled the world from their home on Mount Olympus, the highest mountain in Greece. They watched over the affairs of the world and all human life, keeping the workings of nature regular and ordered.

As the highest mountain in Greece, Mount Olympus was the obvious choice as the home of the gods.

This vase shows the extraordinary birth of Athena, fully-armed, from the head of Zeus.

Twelve all-Greek gods

The twelve most important gods were called the Olympians. Though there were older gods, the Titans, and many other local ones, the Olympians were important all-Greek gods from early times.

It was not always the same twelve gods who were listed as Olympians, but usually they were: Zeus, his wife Hera and his daughter Athena, goddess of wisdom; Poseidon the sea god; Apollo and his sister Artemis; Demeter, goddess of fertility; Hermes, the messenger-god; Aphrodite, goddess of beauty and desire; Ares, god of war; Hephaestus, god of crafts and Hestia, goddess of the hearth. Sometimes Dionysus, god of wine, was listed as an Olympian instead of Hestia. Hades, too, was an important god, but he ruled in the Underworld.

Super beings

To the Greeks, gods were like humans, but more magnificent. Their superhuman qualities – of courage, skill and intelligence – were for people to imitate. But these wonderful super beings also fell in love and fought each other. Even then, they did not suffer pain, or die, as they did not have blood in their bodies, but divine ichor.

This vase shows a sleepy Hephaestus returning to Olympus. He had quarrelled with his mother, Hera, but Dionysus 'persuaded' him to go back by making him drunk.

THEIR OWN WORDS

In Homer's *Iliad*, which tells of the war between the Greeks and Trojans, the Greek warrior Diomedes wounds the goddess Aphrodite, who is on the Trojans' side: *'Diomedes' weapon penetrated her skin through the divine garment, and above the wrist of the god immortal ichor gushed out from her veins... A flow of ichor affected her no more than a flow of tears would, for the gods, who eat no bread and drink no wine, are bloodless and immortal.'*

Gods might shower human beings with gifts, or bring harm to them, depending on how they behaved. Gods sometimes appeared on earth so they seemed close in some ways, but they were also 'above it all'.

Homer told how the gods took sides in the Trojan War. Here Athena helps the Greek Ajax (left), and Apollo supports the Trojan Hector (right).

GODS OF EARTH, SEA AND SKY

The ancient Greeks believed that the gods supervised earth, sea and sky, and all human life. Each god had responsibility for different things.

A stern 5th-century BC bronze head of Zeus, from his sanctuary at Olympia.

enthusiasm: This comes from the Greek words for god, *theos*, and *en*, in. The person who was *entheos* was possessed by a god. So enthusiasm originally meant being possessed by a god.

Zeus and his brothers

The physical world and the Underworld were looked after by Zeus and his two brothers, Poseidon and Hades. In myth, the world had all been shared out between them when the Olympians first came to rule it. All three brothers shared rule over the earth itself, but the rest was divided between them.

Zeus controlled the heavens. He was the sky god, the source of light. The sky and its moods were in his control. He sent clear, calm skies or wind and storms. The thunderbolt was his weapon, and even a nod of his head could shake Mount Olympus.

Ruler of the oceans

From his gold palace under the sea, Poseidon was believed to rule oceans, lakes and rivers. When he shook the earth with his trident, the earth rocked and quaked. Driving a chariot pulled by foaming horses, he roused storms at sea.

A natural-looking bronze of Poseidon, with his trident, from the 2nd century BC.

The ancient Greeks worshipped Zeus on mountain-tops, where sky and earth meet. Zeus controlled the sky, and events in the heavens were signs that could be interpreted by skilful prophets, by 'reading the stars' – the way astrologers still believe they can. And just as people still 'read' hand palms and tea-leaves for signs, the Greeks read the flight of birds, for instance, for signs of the sky-god's intentions: 'flying from right to left to right, if it goes out of sight, it is lucky; but if it raises its left wing… it is unlucky' goes one saying.

A 4th-century BC vase painting of Hades and Persephone, from a Greek colony in Italy.

The zodiac, a Greek word meaning 'circle of animals', was used by the Greeks to divide up the sky and 'read' the stars.

The Underworld

Hades, the third brother, ruled the Underworld, where souls lived after death. He lived there with Persephone, the daughter of Demeter, whom Hades had stolen from her mother. When Persephone is with Hades, flowers wither, nothing grows: winter arrives. When Persephone returns to Demeter, it is spring and flowers bloom again.

The Greeks believed the souls ruled by Hades had, for the most part, a shadowy, silent existence. Some, who had been wicked in life, suffered horrible punishments. A very few others, the good or heroic, went to the Elysian Fields, a land of clear blue skies, where they lived forever in perfect happiness.

GODS of CITY and COUNTRYSIDE

Everywhere, in the cities and in the fields, the Greeks relied on the assistance of the watching gods. At the city's official hearth a fire burned to Hestia, goddess of home and peace.

Protecting the city

Each city also had a protecting patron god. For the city of Corinth it was Poseidon; for Samos, Hera; for Kos, Zeus. No city had the unpopular Ares, the god who loved war. Athens' protector was Athena, goddess of wisdom, who was warlike, but disliked war. She used skill to win battles and to help heroes. She inspired Odysseus to make the Wooden Horse, which the Trojans thought was a gift so they pulled it into Troy, with the Greeks hidden inside.

A relief from Eleusis. A priest is flanked by Demeter (left) and Persephone (right).

A 6th-century BC vase shows Athena in warlike-mode.

The countryside

In the countryside, the skilful Athena took care of groves of olive trees, her gift to Athens. But the most important goddess was Demeter, goddess of agriculture. She made the earth fruitful and taught human beings how to farm. All across Greece women camped out to worship her at the festival of Thesmophoria, while at Eleusis, near Athens, secret torchlight ceremonies, 'mysteries', took place.

A wayside shrine in Greece today, with a picture of a saint and an offering of wine.

By the 5th century AD, belief in the Greek gods had been almost completely swept away by the new religion, Christianity. Some small rituals survived: wayside shrines are still found by the roadsides, although offerings are now made to Jesus, or possibly his mother Mary or the Christian saints. In some parts of Greece, farmers still throw a pomegranate into the soil with the first-sown grain – as if to help release Demeter's daughter, Persephone, from the Underworld. It was because Persephone ate some pomegranate seeds that she had to stay with Hades for part of the year.

panic: Our word 'panic' comes from the name of the Greek countryside god, Pan. In the wilderness he was supposed to inspire a sudden fear that came from nowhere – a pan-ic.

The wilderness

Where ploughed land ended, and forests and mountains began, Apollo and Artemis, twin gods of the sun and moon, looked after the wilderness and wild creatures. Here also a wild goat-footed god, the mischievous Pan, wandered with his pipe, creating sudden terror.

In the countryside too, travellers would add a stone to the wayside cairns placed in honour of Hermes, to ensure a safe journey. Or they might place offerings of food at crossroads for Hecate, the moonlight goddess.

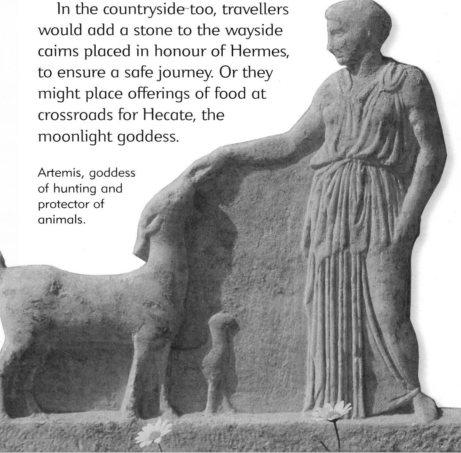

Artemis, goddess of hunting and protector of animals.

11

GODS OF THE HOME

A cluster of gods protected Greek homes. At doorways there was often a small statue to Apollo and a stone Hermes to guard against thieves. Inside, a fire always burned to Hestia, goddess of the hearth.

Protecting the home

In each courtyard there would be an altar to Zeus Herkaois, Zeus of the Enclosure. Zeus had other protecting roles. He had to be honoured as Zeus Georgios, the Farmer, and as Zeus Xenios, Hospitable Zeus, who saw that rules of hospitality were obeyed. He looked after family possessions too, as Zeus Ktesios.

A miniature sculpture of Zeus (14 cm high) from the 4th century BC.

Growing up, love and marriage

Demeter was also important in the home, because as goddess of fruitfulness she helped children grow. As girls left childhood behind them, they dedicated their childhood toys to Artemis, the goddess who looked after young girls. Apollo, her brother, looked after young men.

Each god or goddess had many roles. Artemis not only protected animals but also young girls.

Then when Aphrodite, goddess of desire, entered young people's lives, making them mad with love, they wanted to marry. Aphrodite was a goddess to be feared and honoured; she had made Helen of Troy leave her husband — so starting the Trojan War. But like the equally dangerous Dionysus (see page 15), she was necessary. And Hera, goddess of marriage, was important too; she was called 'the Complete One' because her ideal marriage to Zeus helped her to make men's and women's lives 'complete' in marriage.

This 5th-century BC vase shows the preparations for a wedding.

Aphrodite, said to be the most beautiful goddess.

Family prosperity

The ancient Greeks believed that the gods contributed to family prosperity. The skill of Athena, as goddess of wisdom, was needed for successful weaving, and for the olive harvest. And farm implements could not be made well without the care of Hephaestus, god of metal-working. A household could not be run successfully without honouring its gods.

■■■ LEGACY ■■■

Artists down the ages have painted and sculpted Aphrodite and her attendant Eros. In Greek art, Eros was shown wingless at first, as a young adult. Later Greek artists gave him a bow — to shoot arrows of love. Then the Romans made him into a pudgy baby, and called him Cupid. It is this baby Cupid who fires arrows from St Valentine's Day cards today.

A statue of Eros shoots his arrows in Piccadilly, London.

GODS OF SKILL AND KNOWLEDGE

The Greeks believed that the gods gave different kinds of knowledge. Zeus's favourite son, the sun god Apollo, shot arrows of sunlight to earth along with the light of knowledge. He taught humans prophecy, medicine, art and music.

Apollo

Apollo also revealed things usually hidden from humans. At Delphi, his priests might tell them the plans of the gods. Apollo knew the mysteries of the body, too; he was a healing god, who released humans from pain, and protected nature. But he could send disease to the wicked; sudden deaths were 'the arrows of Apollo'.

Hephaestus and fire

The ancient Greeks believed that the gods gave them technical knowledge. Hephaestus was their fire god; his knowledge was of fire and the crafts of fire. In his volcano-forge (*hephaestos* means fire or volcano) Hephaestus made things for the gods: bronze palaces, the gold watch-dog of Zeus and the arrows of Apollo and Artemis.

Bronze of Apollo from c. 500 BC. He was usually shown as a handsome youth.

Many believed Hephaestus's forge was in the volcano, Mount Etna in Italy.

Hermes and the lyre

Hermes was the cunning street-wise god. On the first morning of his life, he made the first lyre from a tortoise shell, and stole five of Apollo's cattle and cooked one. He became a guardian of wandering things — cattle, merchants, the wind — and travelled on winged sandals with the gods' messages. Invisible in his dog-skin helmet, travelling by night and spinning lies, he was god of thieves and cheats, too — while also protecting people against them.

Apollo's stolen oxen. The hare suggests the speed and craft of the thief, Hermes.

THEIR OWN WORDS

In a famous play by Euripides, the chorus describes how women leave their houses to worship Dionysus in the countryside:

'The whole land is dancing…
In the mountains the dancing
women are rebelling against
spinning and weaving, answering
Dionysus's call.'

pile: Hephaestus, god of fire, had a hat called a *pilos* – a woollen covering. We get the word 'pile' from it – meaning a heap, or the pile of a carpet.

The Greeks enjoyed drinking wine together, which made Dionysus a very popular god.

Dionysus and wine

The last of the Greeks' god-teachers was Dionysus. When the Greeks discovered how to make wine, they thought of it as his gift, although they also recognized its dangers. So, prayers and sacrifices were made to Dionysus around the time of the grape harvest.

15

HEROES

The ancient Greeks honoured 'heroes' as well as gods. Heroes were dead men and women who had done amazing or memorable things.

The cult of the hero

A hero was someone to look up to and to copy, standing as an example of brave and honourable behaviour. Heroes may have originally been real people but, over time, their lives and exploits became the stuff of legend.

A carved gemstone showing Herakles fighting the Lion of Nemea.

Herakles

Like many heroes, Herakles was believed to be the child of a god and a human being. He had super-human supernatural powers but he was a unique hero. Other heroes were mortal, and died; Herakles was rewarded for his brave actions by being made a god, so he would never die.

Sometimes the Greeks were not sure which he really was. A travel writer, Pausanias, describes how at Sikyon worshippers offered Herakles 'a hero's rites', but then 'they sacrifice lambs to him and burn the thighs as if he were a god'.

Local heroes

Herakles was worshipped across the Greek world. Most heroes were local, each city honouring its own. The Athenians held a festival for Theseus. Stories about him told how he made Athens safe for its people, killing the Minotaur and criminal monsters, such as Sinis, who murdered travellers.

This 5th-century BC vase picture shows Theseus killing the giant Sinis.

■■■**LEGACY**■■■

The Greek heroes' superhuman qualities have survived into hundreds of modern super-hero stories. After 2500 years, the stories of Herakles, Theseus and Odysseus continue to be told in books, films, comic strips and plays the world over. The action heroes of today, such as Batman and Superman, have much in common with their ancient ancestors.

Asclepius, with his daughter Hygeia (Health) receives offerings from the sick.

the Milky Way: In one story about Herakles, it says that his father Zeus somehow tricked Hera (who was not his mother) into feeding him. When she realized this, she hurled the baby Herakles away, spilling her milk across the sky. The drops of milk became the galaxy of stars we call the 'Milky Way'.

Cultural heroes

The healer Asclepius — said to be the son of Apollo and a woman — was worshipped first as a hero. He became famous, and was then spoken of as a god. He had large sanctuaries at Epidaurus and several other places. Many of the sick who visited these 'hospitals' claimed to have been cured, having seen the god in a dream and been given his advice.

17

SANCTUARIES AND TEMPLES

The Greeks kept certain places sacred for gods and heroes. They called them sanctuaries and they could be anywhere, on a mountain top, in a deep valley or by a spring or lake.

Even the gods had to perform acts of worship. Here Artemis and Apollo make an offering on an altar to Zeus.

Temples take form

At the heart of the sanctuary was the altar, where animals were sacrificed. At first an altar was a rock or heap of stones, or just a mound of ash piled up from sacrifices.

After about 800 BC, sanctuaries were usually walled, with altars of brick or stone. Small temples began to be built inside the sanctuary. At first they were built of mud-brick and wood. Then from about the 7th century BC, stone was used. Some early temples were only about 30 metres long. But later, huge stone temples were erected, some of which still stand today.

Temple remains in the sanctuary of Apollo on the island of Cyprus.

Sacred statues

Temples were gods' houses on earth and the image of the god would be inside, made of wood or stone. A statue was often brought outside the temple at festivals but some were far too large for that. There was a huge gold-and-ivory statue of Zeus at Olympia that stood 13 metres high!

A drawing of the great statue of Zeus at Olympia, based on a description written by Pausanias.

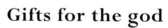

■■■ L E G A C Y ■■■

The Romans often took over Greek temples for their own worship, and built new ones in a mainly Greek style. Then when the Romans became Christian, some temples became churches (including the Parthenon in Athens) or occasionally fragments of the old buildings were re-used in new churches. When interest in the ancient Greeks revived in the 18th century, architects turned to the Greek temple style for inspiration.

This Roman coin celebrates the Greek sanctuary to Artemis (called Diana by the Romans) at Ephesus. It shows a classic temple shape, with the goddess at its centre.

Gifts for the god

All kinds of gifts were dedicated to gods and left in temples: small statues, drinking cups and plates, lyres, even chariots. Sometimes special 'treasuries' had to be built to store them.

Temples were not 'places of worship', like churches. Religious festivals took place in the open air, near the altar. Except at festivals, temples were often locked and closed to visitors. There was rich treasure to protect, and some kinds of worship were secret anyway.

PRIESTS AND ORACLES

A Greek city had many sanctuaries and temples, both inside the city walls and out in the country. They all needed looking after. Priests were the people who did this. Usually men looked after a male god's sanctuary, women a goddess's.

A priest and his helper light the altar fire.

The priest's work

Being a priest was a job to which citizens were elected by the people's council, or chosen by lottery. Priests were not specially trained, but were probably given instructions by the previous one.

Priests had to know exactly what the sacred customs were and settle disagreements about the right way to perform rituals. In addition, the priests kept buildings painted and in good repair. They received festival offerings, helped at sacrifices, sang prayers and made sure sacred rules were not broken.

This early painting (c. 1500 BC) shows a priestess with a sacrificial gift.

THEIR OWN WORDS

An inscription from 306 BC tells us how a sanctuary for a local hero, Egretes, was run by the priest:

'Gods, this sanctuary is rented to Diagnetos for 10 years, for 200 drachmas each year. He has to manage the sanctuary and the buildings, and whitewash the walls...When worshippers sacrifice, he must open the building where the shrine is, ... the kitchen and dining-room.'

These duties were usually written on stone slabs. One inscription says that the priest had to visit every three days and attend for ten days each month. The work brought privileges – a good theatre seat or double portions of festival meat, for example.

prophet: This word comes from the Greek *prophitis*, someone who foretells things, from *pro* – before – and *phimi* - say.

Priestesses put garlands round the necks of two bulls before sacrificing them.

Oracles

There was also a special kind of priest known as an 'oracle'. The oracle was appointed to answer questions addressed through him or her to a god. These special priests often belonged to a particular family or group. The oracle of Zeus at Dodona was in the hands of a tribe called the Selloi.

At Dodona, Zeus' voice was heard at first in the whispering leaves of a huge oak tree. In later times, his message was interpreted from the clink of kettles hanging in the wind.

DELPHI

For the Greeks, the most important oracle was at Delphi, in the sanctuary of Apollo, god of prophecy. By the 7th century BC, a fine temple had been built there, and the Pythian Games were held in honour of Apollo.

A bronze incense burner from the temple of Apollo at Delphi.

The tragic hero Oedipus presents gifts to Apollo at Delphi. The oracle tells him that he will kill his father and marry his mother.

thesaurus: We use the word 'thesaurus' for a kind of dictionary, a store of information. We have taken it from the Greek word *thesauros*, treasure.

The Sacred Precinct

A *gymnasion*, a stadium, and a theatre were part of the sacred site. 'Treasuries', small temple-like buildings, held the gifts of many cities. Inside the temple of Apollo was the oracle, a priestess who was called the Pythia. People came to Delphi from across the Greek world and beyond to seek her advice.

Many questions were asked about city-state affairs — about colonies, war, agriculture and so on. In the 7th century BC, the Spartans asked the oracle whether their new laws were good laws. Yes, was the answer. The people of Thera, after seven years of drought, were told to found a colony in North Africa.

The priestess

Books used to say that the Pythia sat on a stool over a deep hole in the ground which gave off heady fumes; that she ranted her answers in a gibberish which a priest translated into verse. The hole hasn't been found; the raving might have been imagined, but priests wrote down her answers, which often needed interpreting.

One kind of answer did not need interpretation. If a straightforward question was asked: 'Shall we found a new colony?' the reply was either the white bean (yes) or the black bean (no) that the Pythia drew from a jar.

The decline of Delphi

The oracle continued to operate right through the Roman era but the new religion of Christianity led to its end. In the 4th century AD, when the Roman emperor Julian visited Delphi, he was told: 'Apollo no longer has a sanctuary here. The temple has fallen, there are no prophecies. Even the talkative water has dried up.'

This Victorian illustration is a dramatic, if largely inaccurate, reconstruction of consulting the Pythia.

THEIR OWN WORDS

Herodotus tells how King Croesus of Lydia sent messengers to Delphi to ask whether he should attack Persia.

'The oracle told Croesus that if he attacked Persia he would destroy a great empire. Croesus interpreted the oracle as meaning that he would destroy the Persian empire, but it was his own empire that he destroyed.'

Delphi's many buildings and temples climb up a steep mountainside.

CUSTOMS AND RITUALS

The ancient Greeks remembered the gods every day. Before drinking wine, for instance, they poured a small amount on the ground; this was an offering – a libation – to a god.

Prayer and sacrifice

Libations were poured before the Assembly began, before and after journeys, and so on. It was a ritual – a regular action that was a way of showing respect to a god. Prayer was another ritual. The Greeks prayed anytime, anywhere, and made up their own prayers.

A priestess pours a libation for a worshipper.

Gifts for the gods

The most important ritual was sacrifice. Sacrifice means giving up something, and one common offering was food – cakes, corn, wine, honey and figs. Often this was the first part of a crop or of someone's work, called 'first-fruits'. Small statues were popular as first-fruits. One on the Acropolis in Athens has this dedication on its base: 'The potter Nearchos dedicated me to Athena as first-fruit of his work. Antenor made me.' Such gifts might be in gratitude for a piece of luck or they might be in the hope of a return favour.

This small statue of a young woman making a sacrifice was probably an offering itself.

Sacrificing animals

Those gift-sacrifices were 'bloodless', but some sacrifices involved killing and cooking animals and offering part of them. The Greeks usually did not eat meat except on these occasions. They sacrificed domestic animals, such as pigs, sheep and goats, and then ate them. The gods, strangely, were offered the 'nasty' bits — bones, innards and burnt thigh-pieces. This was because, long ago, the gods had been tricked into choosing the wrong portion. But the Greeks believed the gods did not eat human food anyway, though they loved the smells that rose from the fire to heaven.

This 5th-century BC vase painting shows blood-stained priests sacrificing an animal.

THEIR OWN WORDS

A Greek poet on his travels wrote down this prayer to Hermes as a not-very-serious poem:

'Please Hermes, I'm praying to you because I'm shivering and frozen. Get me, Hipponax, a nice woollen overcoat, a Persian cape and some felt slippers. This cold's rattling my teeth!'

This 4th-century BC carving shows a whole family coming to sacrifice a ram to Dionysus.

FESTIVALS AND CELEBRATIONS

Greek life was full of festivals, public and private. Athens had as many as 120 public festival days a year, with processions, dancing, music and sacrifices.

The Athenian processions often led to the Parthenon, the great temple at Athens' centre.

City festivals

Festivals often included games. Anything that the Greeks strove to do well in — music, athletics, dancing, weaving — they competed in. Among the competitions were ones for male beauty, dancing in armour and dismounting from chariots. Competitors presented the gods with their 'gifts' — the reciter's dramatic skill and memory, the dancer's or athlete's trained body.

Games were always religious, but successful athletes made money. They could win huge amounts of olive oil or valuable gold wreaths.

A procession at Delphi. Apollo sits on the left and a priest greets arriving guests.

Village festivals

The *deme* – or village – had its festivals, like the city, not so large but just as frequent. In Erkhia, just east of Athens, an inscription listing only some of the sacrifices for one year takes up five columns of over sixty lines each, and mentions over forty gods!

In the family

Smaller ceremonies, sometimes with animal sacrifices, took place inside the family, with the head of the family as priest. At weddings, several gods, especially Zeus and Hera Teleia – seen as the ideal married couple – were requested to protect the marriage. Artemis and Demeter were asked to watch over birth. A new baby was carried around the hearth, and on the tenth day, there were sacrifices and a banquet. At death, the soul was given into the care of the gods Hypnos, Sleep, and Thanatos, Death, who took it to the Underworld. The family followed strict rules for mourning their dead.

At festivals large and small, dancing girls 'delighted' the gods.

THEIR OWN
WORDS

This hymn to Apollo describes festival events:
'In remembrance of you the Ionians assemble in their long tunics, with their wives and children. They delight you with boxing, with song and with dancing.'

The tomb of a 4th-century BC prince. At its top is a funerary procession while six 'wailers' or mourners are carved on its side.

ALL-GREEK GAMES

Four great festivals – at Delphi, Nemea, Corinth and Olympia – were pan-Hellenic, or all-Greek; competitors came from anywhere in the Greek world.

The Olympics

The Olympic Games were held in honour of Zeus. They began in 776 BC, lasting one day, and attracting only local people. Later, they went on for several days, with perhaps 40,000 visitors watching trained athletes from all over Greece – but only men; except for one priestess, women couldn't even watch, on pain of death. Younger girls could, though.

An athlete sculpted in bronze wearing a winner's wreath

Athletes entered the stadium at Olympia through a narrow passage.

The first day was for processions, sacrifices and taking oaths. Olympic officials, who also trained the athletes, made sure the religious rules were obeyed. On the second day the athletic events began, including chariot-races, races in armour and the *pankration* (boxing combined with wrestling). Victors were given an olive branch, taken from the sacred grove, and money.

Athletes race across this 6th-century BC vase, itself a prize in a games.

The idea of the Olympic Games was revived in the 19th century, and the first modern Olympics was held in Athens in 1896. Like the original Olympics they are held every four years. Competitors come from every corner of the world. There are many events, but those at the core are Greek: running races, long-jump, discus and javelin.

Music and painting competitions

The Pythian Games at Delphi began as competitions for lyre and kithara, to remember the legend when Apollo killed the serpent Pytho. The Games at Isthmia, near Corinth, in honour of Poseidon, included competitions in speaking and painting.

Winners were given wreaths; at Delphi it was laurel, sacred to Apollo. But though the real prize might be the honour of winning, victors were feted. For one, a stretch of city-wall was specially demolished for him to come home through. Most were rewarded with gifts and money.

A gold medal from the first modern Olympics. The central figure is Athena.

athlete: Our word 'athlete' comes from two Greek words, *athlos*, a prize, and *athlitis*, competing for a prize.

The end of the Games

In 146 BC, Greece became part of the Roman Empire. The Romans tried, unsuccessfully, to transfer the Olympics to Rome. Instead the Olympics, and the other pan-Hellenic games, became local events again, as at the beginning. Finally, in AD 393, the Emperor Thedosius abolished all non-Christian festivals. The Olympics were over – or so it seemed at the time.

GLOSSARY

Ajax: legendary Greek warrior who fought in the Trojan War.

assembly: in Greek city-states, male citizens met in an assembly to argue and decide what laws to pass.

citizen: a recognized member of city-state (unlike foreigners or slaves) with certain rights, e.g. only citizens could own land. Both men and women were citizens, but only men could vote in the assembly.

city: in ancient Greece, cities were the centres of small states. From about 800 to 400 BC, Greece was divided into a series of city-states, each with their own laws and systems of government.

colony: a settlement of people who have left their own homes to live somewhere else. After about 800 BC, Greek cities sent out many citizens to form colonies all around the Mediterranean and Black Sea.

Corinth: one of the leading city-states of ancient Greece, situated west of Athens on the narrow strip of land that joins the Peloponnese to the rest of mainland Greece.

deme: a village and its people.

drachma: the unit in which Greek money is counted, both in ancient and modern Greece.

Elysian Fields: the perfect land where the Greeks believed the souls of people who had lived good or heroic lives travelled after death.

Euripides (c. 485–406 BC): Athenian playwright, famous for his tragedies. His plays, such as *Medea*, are still frequently performed in theatres around the world.

Hector: legendary prince of Troy who led the Trojans against the Greeks and died to save his city.

Herodotus (c. 480-425 BC): sometimes called the first historian, Herodotus wrote about the wars between the Greeks and Persians.

Hesiod (c. 700 BC): Greek poet from whose works we know many of the principal Greek myths.

Homer (c. 8th century BC): the blind poet who composed two great story-poems, *The Iliad* and *The Odyssey*, that were recited and performed in ancient Greece and are still read today.

ichor: the liquid that ran in the gods' veins instead of blood.

Ionians: speakers of one of the major ancient Greek dialects, mainly found in the Aegean Islands and Ionia, a Greek colony on the coast of modern Turkey.

Kos: Greek island off the coast of modern Turkey.

GODS, GODDESSES AND HEROES

The god, goddesses and heroes mentioned in this book are listed here. Their later Roman names are given in brackets.

Aphrodite (Venus): an Olympian, goddess of desire, love and beauty; married to Hephaestus but had other lovers.

Apollo: an Olympian, son of Zeus and Leto, twin brother of Artemis. Perhaps the most important god after Zeus, Apollo was god of the sun and light, archery, poetry and music, healing and prophecy.

Ares (Mars): an Olympian, god of war, son of Zeus and Hera and lover of Aphrodite.

Artemis (Diana): an Olympian, daughter of Zeus and Leto, twin sister of Apollo; a virgin goddess of hunting, protector of wild animals and young girls. She was a goddess of light associated with the moon.

Asclepius (Asculapius): a legendary healer whose status as a hero gradually changed to that of a god of medicine. He was held to be a son of Apollo.

Athena (Minerva): an Olympian, goddess of wisdom and industry (including weaving and olive-growing) and war; daughter of Zeus and the Titan, Metis.

Demeter (Ceres): an Olympian, sister of Zeus; a goddess of nature and farming. Her grief over the loss of her daughter Persephone to Hades caused the seasons.

Dionysus (Bacchus): an Olympian (replacing Hestia), son of Zeus and the mortal Semele; a nature god, particularly associated with wine and later the theatre.

Eros (Cupid): a god of love, son of Aphrodite and (in some accounts) Hermes.

Hades (Dis): god of the Underworld and ruler of the souls of the dead, brother of Zeus. Also known as Pluto.

libation: the first part of a drink, often wine, poured to the ground or on an altar as an offering to a god.

Lydia: a large, civilized country lying behind the coastal Greek settlements in Ionia.

Mycenaean: describes the civilization that existed in Greece from around 1700 BC but seems to have collapsed about 500 years later. Many Greek stories and religious beliefs seem to have originated around this time.

Odysseus: legendary Greek warrior and hero, who fought in the Trojan War. The story of his return from Troy is told in Homer's *Odyssey*.

Oedipus: legendary king of Thebes, whose tragic story was famous in ancient Greece. Separated from his parents at birth, he unknowingly kills his father and marries his mother, as the Delphic oracle prophesied. He blinds himself when he discovers what he has done.

oracle: a priest who answered questions that cities or individuals asked about their futures or about problems they had. The word is also used to mean the answer itself.

Pausanias (c. 2nd century AD): Greek geographer who travelled around Greece and described its principal cities and religious centres in his work *Description of Greece*.

Persian Empire: the great empire to the east of Greece in Asia, which invaded Greece twice in the early 5th century BC.

Pythia: the priestess who gave out the oracles at Delphi.

Samos: Greek island off the coast of Turkey. In ancient times, it was colonized by Ionian Greeks and was a major commercial centre.

sanctuary: a place sacred to a god or goddess with an altar and sometimes a temple.

Sparta: the chief city-state of the Peloponnese, in southern Greece, and often Athens' rival and enemy. Sparta was famed for its tough attitudes. Its people were constantly prepared and ready for war.

treasury: a small temple-like building which housed a city's gifts to a god.

Trojan War: the war between the Greeks and people of Troy (a city whose remains are near the mouth of the Black Sea in modern Turkey). Known through Homer's *Iliad* and long considered legendary, the war is now generally accepted to have taken place c. 1193–1184 BC.

vase: a word used to describe Greek pottery in all its many different shapes and sizes.

Underworld: the shadowy lands beneath the earth, where the Greeks believed most souls went after death. A few heroes' souls went instead to the Elysian Fields.

Hecate: one of the Titans, goddess of the moon, witchcraft and magic.

Hephaestus (Vulcan): an Olympian, son of Zeus and Hera; god of fire and metal crafts. He is said to have been lame.

Hera (Juno): an Olympian, queen of the gods as sister and wife of Zeus; goddess of women, marriage and childbirth.

Herakles (Hercules): hero and later god, son of Zeus and a mortal queen Alcmene.

Hermes (Mercury): an Olympian, son of Zeus and Maia; god of travellers, commerce and thieves; messenger of the gods.

Hestia (Vesta): an Olympian (later giving up her place to Dionysus), sister of Zeus, goddess of the hearth and family.

Hypnos: god of sleep, son of night and twin brother of Thanatos.

Pan: a nature god, son of Hermes and a nymph; he was half-man and half-goat.

Persephone (Prosperina): daugher of Zeus and Demeter; wife of Hades.

Poseidon (Neptune): an Olympian, brother of Zeus; god of the seas, rivers and lakes and also earthquakes.

Thanatos: god of death, son of night and twin brother of Hypnos.

Theseus: legendary king of Athens, who was worshipped there as a hero.

Titans: the gods who ruled the universe before the Olympians, who defeated and imprisoned them. Zeus's and his siblings' parents were the Titans Cronus and Rhea.

Zeus (Jupiter): king of the Gods, an Olympian, brother of Poseidon, Hera, Hades, Hestia and Demeter and father of many deities. Ruler of the heavens and sky. His weapon was the thunderbolt.

INDEX